RE ME

A JOURNEY OF HEALING, DELIVERANCE, & RESTORATION

Dr. Shannon Swiney-Bruce

RE ME: A Journey of Healing, Deliverance, & Restoration

Author Photography by Kimazing Photography LLC
Book Cover Design by Dr. Shannon Swiney-Bruce

POP Journey Publishing
PO Box 32143
Newark NJ 07102
popjourneypublishing@gmail.com

Printed in the United States of America.

Library of Congress Cataloging-in-Publication data

Dedication

This book is dedicated to Dorothy Kettles, a woman God prepared for me.

Mother Kettles has been a blessing in my life since I was a young girl. When God planted her in my ministry, He also deepened our relationship and gave me a new appreciation for the gift of spiritual covering and connection. She has been a source of comfort in my life, faithfully praying for me, encouraging me, and continually reminding me of Scripture and God's unfailing faithfulness.

Most importantly, she has walked with me through my process of restoration. God was my anchor and the wind that kept me from sinking, but she stayed in the ship with me when the boisterous wind came and threatened to destroy me.

Thank you, Mother Kettles, for your steadfastness and diligence in ministry and in my personal life. Thank you for accepting me as a whole person—strengths, weaknesses, and flaws—and for never giving up on me. God will not forget your labor and the love you have shown toward His servant.

I love and appreciate you!

TABLE OF CONTENTS

Introduction:

From Rejection To Restoration

Rejection: the act of refusing to accept, use, or believe someone or something.[1] Throughout my life, rejection showed up in many forms. I was denied access, fellowship, community, and opportunities—not always because I lacked ability but because I did not fit in, did not look the part, or did not meet someone else's standard. At times, I was told I could not be used. Other times, I was simply deemed unqualified.

Instead of resting in who God created me to be, I wrestled to prove people wrong. I became a high achiever to prove I was capable, qualified, and worthy. I sacrificed pieces of myself to gain people's friendship—to belong, be seen, affirmed, and accepted. Those who have suffered rejection and responded in similar ways know exactly what I mean.

Then came the deepest rejection I had ever experienced—one that left me broken. I felt violated and spiritually bankrupt to the point that I could not utter a word for three days. The pain cut so deeply into my soul that I began to believe the lies of the enemy. I agreed with him when he whispered that I was disqualified. I withdrew, isolated myself, and eventually stopped going to church—not because I no longer loved God but because I believed I no longer belonged. I found no nourishment for my faith there, only fuel for more fear.

I convinced myself that if God allowed me to experience such pain, then perhaps He had rejected me too. I believed that the weaknesses my trials exposed somehow disqualified me from the kingdom, that God could no longer use me. For a season, I allowed those lies to bombard my mind unchecked. In my exhaustion, I did nothing. And in that stillness, the enemy led me down a dark path while I was too tired to fight back.

For more than five years, I had endured spiritual warfare, where I was sifted as wheat and taken through a relentless season of trials. The enemy attacked every area of my life, and eventually that onslaught knocked the wind out of me. I was not prepared for the final round. I was so busy doing ministry that I neglected to prepare myself spiritually. I failed to rest, reset, and be still in God's presence for refreshing. I quickly learned that exhaustion is one of the enemy's favorite opportunities.

He came in through distraction, discord, and division, applying pressure until I was numb from the fight. I fought until I had no strength left, and when the final blow came, I gave in. I told myself that if God was not on my side, there was no point in continuing. That surrender cost me dearly. I suffered great loss—emotionally, spiritually, relationally, and financially. I was hurt, depressed, neglected, and deeply wounded in my soul.

When you come into agreement with the enemy's lies, you give him access to everything God blessed you with and never intended you to lose. Little by little, I watched the enemy take what I believed I no longer deserved nor had the strength to fight for. I forgot that while my strength had failed, God's never will. I forgot that Jesus' strength is made perfect in weakness. Though I was weary, God was not. He had already promised to be my rearguard and fight my battles. Even while I sat depressed, faint, and hopeless, God fought for me.

In the midst of everything, I could still feel His presence and His peace. Day after day, I found myself opening the Word of God, hearing the Holy Spirit whisper in a still, small voice, "Keep fighting." Month after month, I struggled to respond in faith, yet God's mercy met me daily. The Holy Spirit comforted me patiently, reminding me that this was not the end.

Through that comfort, revelation came: God would never leave me or forsake me.

Be strong and courageous,
for the LORD your God goes with you.
He will never leave you nor forsake you.
(Deuteronomy 31:6 NIV)

He said,

"Shannon, *Fear not, for I am with you. ...*
I will uphold you with My righteous right hand."
(Isaiah 41:10 NKJV)

And He did exactly that. He sat and waited with me, caught my tears, felt my pain, and held me up with His righteous right hand. Although I was only going through the motions, I continued to seek Him and sit quietly in

His presence. And the Holy Spirit reminded me of this truth:

In John 6:37, Jesus says,

> "*Those the Father has given me will come to me, and I will never reject them.*" (NLT)

That's when I finally broke my silence and asked God to "Re Me." I cried out from the deep depths of my soul with a loud voice: "Abba Father, If I find favor in Your sight, please Re Me. I need You, Father, to Re Me."

He heard, and He answered.

Why This Book Exists

This book exists for healing, deliverance, and restoration. It is written for those who have been wounded by rejection, exhausted by striving, silenced by fear, or disconnected from their true identity in God. It is for those who love God but feel lost, those who served faithfully but burned out quietly, and those who wonder if their failures or weaknesses have disqualified them from purpose.

I want to be clear. This is not a book of perfection. It is a book of process. I encourage you to be open to and to embrace the process.

Each chapter walks through a divine RE: repent, redeem, refine, revive, reinstall, reset, reclaim, realign, and restore—revealing how God patiently rebuilds what trauma, betrayal, and spiritual warfare tried to destroy. This journey is not about returning to who you were but discovering who you were always created to be.

WHO THIS BOOK IS FOR

This book is for anyone who:

- Has struggled with rejection or identity confusion
- Has grown weary in faith or ministry
- Has survived spiritual warfare without understanding what happened
- Is ready to stop surviving and begin living whole
- Desires divine alignment with God, not religious performance

You do not need to have all the answers. You only need a willing heart.

AN INVITATION

If you have ever cried out, "God, I need You to re me," this journey is for you.

Let this book walk with you from brokenness to wholeness—not by rushing the process but by honoring it. God is not finished with you. He never was and never will be.

How To Use This Book

This book is written to be read slowly and prayerfully. Some chapters may stir memories, emotions, or questions. That is part of the healing process. Allow the Holy Spirit to guide you as you read. Pause when necessary and breathe through the emotions. Reflect on memories and rephrase as often as needed, using the Word of God. Return to prayer when questions arise.

Restoration does not happen in one moment; it unfolds over time.

DEFINITION

Re is a prefix defined by Merriam-Webster as "again, anew, back, backward: recall."[2]

Re defined by Membean: "Prefixes are key morphemes in English vocabulary that begin words. The prefix **re**, which means "back" or "again," appears in hundreds of English vocabulary words, for example: **re**ject, **re**generate, and **re**vert. You can remember that the prefix **re** means 'back' via the word **re**turn or turn 'back.' To remember that **re** means 'again,' consider **re**arrange or arrange 'again.' For example, 'when you **re**ject a plan, you throw it back.' Or when you are **re**turning home from an outing, you are turning 'back' home.'"[3]

This book is the story of how God restored me.

CHAPTER ONE: REPENT

TURNING BACK TO GOD

Rejection had been a constant battle in my life. From an early age, it shaped how I showed up in the world and how I interacted with others. I learned quickly that approval felt like safety and being needed felt like belonging. Over time, my desire to be accepted became a pattern of people-pleasing. I prioritized the needs of others over my own at the expense of my voice, my boundaries, and my peace. I feared rejection, confrontation, and conflict, and I carried a deep need for validation from people. I did not realize then that my fear of rejection was quietly replacing my trust in God. I was seeking affirmation from people for what only God could provide. And the problem with seeking approval from others is this: It eventually leads to disobeying God.

Disobedience creates distance—not because God withdraws but because alignment is broken. Scripture clearly illustrates this in the story of Adam and Eve.

When they ate from the Tree of the Knowledge of Good and Evil, they lost their innocence and became aware of their nakedness. That exposure symbolized the cost of disobedience: Shame, fear, guilt, and insecurity entered where trust once lived.

Having lost everything I worked so hard for, I found myself broken and remorseful. My finances were gone. My marriage was fractured. My ministry had shut down. Most painfully, my relationship with God felt distant.

For a season, I blamed others. But blame has an expiration date. When I reached the bottom, I had no one left to point to but myself. I took full responsibility for my choices and repented. I acknowledged that I had walked by sight instead of by faith, trusted people over God, and followed voices that did not align with His truth. True repentance makes no excuses, assigns no blame, and does not dwell in self-hate.

REPENTANCE DEFINED

Repentance is a private meeting with God where truth is spoken without blame-shifting. It is facing reality, owning responsibility, accepting consequences, and turning fully back toward Him. It is releasing others and even God from responsibility for the decisions we have made. Repentance is a complete about-face into alignment with God.

Merriam-Webster defines *repent* as to "feel sorrow, regret or contrition" about one's wrongdoing or sin."[4] To repent is to experience a change of heart and mind, to turn away from sin and turn back toward God. Repentance is not self-condemnation; it is realignment. Healing and restoration always begin at repentance. God's promise in 2 Chronicles 7:14 says,

If my people, who are called by my name,
will humble themselves
and pray and seek my face
and turn from their wicked ways,
then I will hear from heaven, and I will forgive
their sin and will heal their land. (NIV)

The Desire of Thought

Through my trials, I learned that the real battle is not simply between flesh and spirit, but between "the desire of thought" and "God's plan." The enemy works by introducing thoughts that stir desire outside of God's will, baiting us to question what God has already given.

Genesis 3 shares with us the story of the fall of mankind. The scene shows us the conversation between the serpent and the woman. We may look at it as a story, but it reveals the blueprint of the battle between the desire of thought and God's plan for mankind. Also, this account reveals the enemy's method of baiting believers to rob them of God's plan and purpose for their lives. The enemy uses a four-step method: bait, doubt, desire, and curiosity.

The serpent asked the woman a question, "*Did God really say, 'You must not eat from any tree in the garden'?*" (NIV). This is what you call "bait." He used the question to bait her. She responded to the serpent, "*We may eat fruit from the trees in the garden, but God did say, 'You must not eat fruit from the tree that is in the middle of the garden, and you must not touch it, or you will die'*" (NIV).

The serpent countered, "*You will not certainly die*" (NIV). This statement opened the door for doubt and confusion, which activates the "desire of thought."

The serpent then said, "*For God knows that when you eat from it your eyes will be opened, and you will be like God, knowing good and evil*" (NIV). This statement initiated the "curiosity of thought," which led Eve to the bait.

When the woman saw that the fruit of the tree was good for food and pleasing to the eye, and also desirable for gaining wisdom, she took some and ate it.
(Genesis 3:6 NIV)

As soon as Eve ate the bait, her eyes were opened, and she realized she was naked. She disobeyed God and opened the door for sin. In that moment, she recognized that she was exposed, uncovered, and void of something. In reality, God had given Adam and Eve everything they needed, but due to sin, they were no longer in alignment with God. Their sin opened the door for mental, physical, emotional, and spiritual attacks. The impact of every attack weakens the faith of the believer.

Unfortunately, the enemy baited me the same way, by influencing me to desire what I thought I did not have: love, acceptance, approval. I sought approval and acceptance from people when I already had acceptance, love, and approval from God.

TURNING BACK

When I finally turned back to God, He did not condemn me. He answered with peace—a peace that surpassed all understanding. In that peace, I knew that though I had disappointed Him, God had not abandoned me. He reminded me of His mercy and how I was made righteous through Jesus. A righteousness I did not have to earn because Jesus had already secured it for me:

God made him who had no sin to be sin for us,
so that in him we might become
the righteousness of God.
(2 Corinthians 5:21 NIV)

Repentance is often misunderstood as punishment, humiliation, or proof of failure. However, the truth is repentance is none of those things. Repentance is an invitation, an invitation to return to alignment with God without shame. Disobedience does not create distance because God withdraws; it creates distance because alignment is broken. When Adam and Eve ate from the Tree of the Knowledge of Good and Evil, shame entered where trust once lived. God did not abandon them; He came looking for them, and He clothed them. When I turned back to God in honesty and transparency, He clothed me and reminded me of His Word.

It is written that Jesus had already redeemed me, a love offering that cannot be undone. I had never fallen from grace; I needed to reconnect to it.

*****

Reflection

What is God showing me?
What did God reveal to me through this chapter?
What area of my heart, thinking, or behavior is He inviting me to bring into alignment?

Biblical Truth to Carry

If we confess our sins, He is faithful and just to forgive us our sins and to cleanse us from all unrighteousness. (1 John 1:9 NKJV)

CLOSING PRAYER

Abba Father,

Thank You for revealing truth to my heart and for meeting me where I am. Thank You for drawing me and allowing me into Your presence. I surrender my life fully to You and ask You to forgive me for not trusting You. Heal what has been wounded by my own choices and misunderstandings. Realign my heart with Your will and help me walk in obedience and trust You in every area of my life. I receive Your mercy, grace, and restoration today. In the name of Jesus, amen.

Chapter Two: Redeemed

The Work of Redemption

After acknowledging my mistakes and turning back to God, I felt a weight lift that I had not even realized I was carrying. I had believed my failures disqualified me, but God whispered a truth I had almost forgotten: I am redeemed. I am chosen. I am His.

Redeem is defined as the act of buying back, restoring, or reclaiming what was lost.[5] After a season of disobedience and loss, I realized that God's work in my life had never been about my failures. It was always about His faithfulness. Even when I stumbled, even when I thought I had ruined everything, God's redemptive work had already reclaimed my identity, my purpose, and my life.

My debt was already cleared. Scripture tells us,

In Him we have redemption through His blood,
the forgiveness of sins,

according to the riches of His grace.
(Ephesians 1:7 NKJV)

Through Jesus Christ, the debt of sin—past, present, and future—has already been paid.

Yet the enemy's assignment is to confuse believers into thinking that disobedience, failure, or bondage has disqualified them from God's grace. In my case, after enduring prolonged spiritual attacks and suffering a deep soul injury, the enemy used lies to convince me I had done something so severe that God could not forgive me. This is how captivity begins through deception.

After taking hit after hit in spiritual warfare, I was emotionally exhausted and spiritually weary. I forgot what Jesus had already accomplished for me. I forgot who I was in Christ. But even in my weakness, God never left the battlefield. He continued to fight for me even after I had thrown in the towel. He continued to remind me that He had healed and restored me, that I was already redeemed.

That is the beauty hidden within trials and tribulations: The work has already been done. Jesus secured the victory long before I reached the battlefield. His sacrifice was eternal, reconciling us to the Father once and for all. Redemption does not require striving; it requires repentance, surrender, and trust.

True surrender is the complete release of control into the Father's hands. I knew I needed rescue, and more than anything, I desired perfect alignment with my Abba Father. For me, being out of alignment with God, even for a short time, is like living a lifetime in the desert without water. Through scripture, the Holy Spirit guided me back to trust:

Commit your way to the LORD;
trust in him, and he will act.
(Psalm 37:5 ESV)

When I chose to trust God with my whole heart and lean not on my own understanding, He began to straighten my path (Proverbs 3:5–6). When I sought His kingdom first, He faithfully provided everything else (Matthew 6:33).

I surrendered everything—my plans, my expectations, my wounds—and allowed the Holy Spirit full control. The Spirit guided me step by step, reminding me that because of Jesus' sacrifice, I had full access to the presence of God.

Let us then approach God's throne of grace
with confidence,
so that we may receive mercy
and find grace to help us in our time of need.
(Hebrews 4:16 NIV)

In response, I withdrew from the noise of social media, gatherings, people, places, and distractions and entered the secret place with the Father. The secret place became my refuge. It was the only place where I felt safe enough to be restored, protected, and refined. The term *secret place* comes from the Hebrew root word *cether*, meaning "to hide" or "to be concealed."[6] I said to God, *You are my hiding place; you will protect me from trouble and surround me with songs of deliverance* (Psalm 32:7 NIV). God became my hiding place. In that place, there was no striving—only worship, stillness, and receiving.

There was no need for excessive talking because God already knew what was depleted within me before I had the words to ask. Jesus said, "*Your Father knows what you need before you ask him*" (Matthew 6:8 NIV). For months, I remained in the secret place worshiping, waiting, and allowing God to rebuild what had been broken.

And in that sacred stillness, God reconnected me to the truth of redemption. I came to full agreement with this truth: God says, "*I am God, and there is no other; I am God, and there is none like me*" (Isaiah 46:9 NIV). God's redemption is not conditional on our performance; it is anchored in His character. No matter how far we've strayed, what we've lost, or how broken we feel, we are already redeemed. Redemption is God's act of restoring value and identity. It is a gift freely given, not earned. The revelation of redemption restored my access to the Father by faith, but the secret place prepared me for what came next.

*****

Reflection

What is God showing me?
What did God reveal to me through this chapter?
What area of my heart, thinking, or behavior is He inviting me to bring into alignment?

BIBLICAL TRUTH TO CARRY

In Him we have redemption through His blood, the forgiveness of sins, according to the riches of His grace. (Ephesians 1:7 NKJV)

CLOSING PRAYER

Abba Father,
Thank You for purchasing me with Your precious blood and meeting me where I am. Thank You for revealing truth to my heart and helping me to see my worth through Your eyes. I accept your gift of debt cancellation and liberty. Realign my heart with Your will and help me live life as a free woman, in obedience and faith. In the name of Jesus, amen.

Chapter Three: Refined

The Fire and the Press

Refining is the process of removing impurities or unwanted elements from a substance—to purify and to improve the quality of something by subjecting it to fire and pressure. It is used to mature the believer, removing weak character traits, double-mindedness, and sinful behaviors. I had allowed so much of what was not God to come in that I needed refining. The Bible lets us know that God is a consuming fire, and I desired for everything that was not God to be burned out. In Zechariah 13:9, God says,

> "*I will bring that group through the fire*
> *and make them pure.*
> *I will refine them like silver*
> *and purify them like gold.*
> *They will call on my name, and I will answer them.*
> *I will say, 'These are my people,'*
> *and they will say, 'The LORD is our God.'*" (NLT)

Our Abba Father wants us to look only to Him as the LORD our God. He is a jealous God. When we replace Him with the world system and the people of the world, then refinement and realignment are necessary.

At the time I did not understand, but I now know that God was calling me deeper into a relationship with Him and preparing me for the next phase of my life. Scripture often refers to this process as pruning. In John 15:2, Jesus explains that the Father prunes us so we may continue to bear fruit. He says,

> "*Every branch in Me that does not bear fruit He takes away; and every branch that bears fruit He prunes, that it may bear more fruit.*" (NKJV)

Through my own life experiences, I came to understand that fruit-bearing is a cut-and-grow process we will undergo multiple times throughout our lives.

I want to be honest: There was a time when I ran from the pruning process because I did not recognize it for what it was. Like many others, I believed pruning meant I had done something wrong, that God was stripping me as punishment. But that mindset is rooted in religion not relationship. Religion causes fear and assumes punishment; a relationship teaches us to trust God through the process as He reveals purpose.

In the secret place, I learned that God uses trials, testing, and even suffering—not to harm His children but to refine them. When we resist or run from pruning, the process is prolonged and becomes more painful than necessary. No one is exempt from pruning. Whenever the Father intends to elevate us, refinement must come first.

God has already established this order. When His Word was spoken, it was settled. In a healthy relationship with the Father, there is no fear, only peace. Even in refinement, we can trust Him to lead us safely through the pruning and know that His grace is sufficient.

Rooted to Grow

Pruning is not optional; it is necessary. God often compares us to trees—living organisms meant to grow, bear fruit, and remain rooted. Jeremiah 17:8 says:

> *For he shall be like a tree planted by the waters,*
> *which spreads out its roots by the river,*
> *and will not fear when heat comes;*
> *but its leaf will be green,*

and will not be anxious in the year of drought,
nor will it cease from yielding fruit. (NKJV)

This imagery reveals several truths. Trees represent life, and water is essential to sustain that life. For us, the Word of God and the Holy Spirit represent water for nourishment. Trees can grow hundreds of feet tall, but without deep roots, they cannot withstand storms or heat. Roots anchor the tree, providing stability, nourishment, and balance. When we are grounded and rooted in God's Word, we do not fear when the heat of life increases. Trials do not stop our growth; instead, they deepen our roots.

THE PAIN OF LETTING GO

Before stepping into new levels, we must grow in character, integrity, wisdom, and strength. That growth often requires separation from people, places, habits, and attachments we have grown comfortable with. This is why many run from refinement; letting go hurts.

I reached a point where my well was dry. I was no longer bearing fruit. I was exhausted and frustrated, operating on fumes. I knew I needed rest, but instead of stopping, I kept going, against wisdom, until I burned out. Exhaustion created an open door for the enemy. Weariness is one of his greatest opportunities. However, I thank God for His lovingkindness toward us that even in pruning, He is gentle.

Pruned with Precision

I once heard an illustration that stayed with me. On the TV show *This Old House*, a tree expert explained that pruning must be done the right way or it can cause long-term damage. A single careless cut can tear bark, leaving wounds that take much longer to heal.

He demonstrated a three-cut method—careful, intentional, and precise—so the tree could heal properly. He said,

> Make an undercut about a foot away from where the branch meets the trunk. This cut should only go about a third of the way through the branch. Make a second cut from the top down, an inch or two further out than the first cut and continue cutting until the branch breaks free. Make a final cut.[7]

That illustration reminded me of God's wisdom in pruning us. When we try to prune our own lives, we often cut from what is visible, removing what feels painful or uncomfortable. In one single cut, we remove what has caused us pain or discomfort. But God sees beneath the surface. His pruning is intentional and restorative, never reckless. But His cuts allow us to heal properly and on time.

Scripture reminds us that refinement has purpose:

> *Our present sufferings are not worth comparing with the glory that will be revealed in us.*
> (Romans 8:18 NIV)

> *We ... are being transformed into [His] image from glory to glory.*
> (2 Corinthians 3:18 NKJV)

When we experience spiritual decline, God refines us—not to condemn us but to reconnect us to our first love. We did not choose Him; He first loved us. Separation from the Father leads to decline, but refinement restores life. To God be the glory for His mercy that He refines us, revives us, and reconnects us to the life He died for us to have.

Reflection

What is God showing me?
What did God reveal to me through this chapter?
What area of my heart, thinking, or behavior is He inviting me to bring into alignment?

Biblical Truth to Carry

God says, "*I will bring that group through the fire and make them pure. I will refine them like silver and purify them like gold. They will call on my name, and I will answer them. I will say, 'These are my people,' and they will say, 'The LORD is our God.'*"

(Zechariah 13:9 NLT)

Closing Prayer

Abba Father,
Thank You for refining and purifying me. Thank You for pruning me that I may continue to bear fruit for You. In the name of Jesus, amen.

Chapter Four: Revived

Breath and Life Restored

Revival is the restoration of life, consciousness, strength, and vigor.[8] When a believer suffers a soul injury, falls away, or becomes overwhelmed by the enemy, they lose God-consciousness. In that unconscious state, stagnation sets in, clarity fades, strength weakens, joy diminishes, peace disappears, and identity becomes blurred. Scripture describes this condition clearly: *They are darkened in their understanding and separated from the life of God because of the ignorance that is in them due to the hardening of their hearts* (Ephesians 4:18 NIV).

Disobedience and ignorance of God's Word create distance, dull spiritual awareness, and lead to disconnection from God. When this happens, revival is necessary, and I needed revival.

Refined and Focused

Revival begins when we refocus on God through His Word, prayer, and worship. This is the work of the Holy Spirit to awaken, realign, and restore. Peter said,

> *"Repent therefore and be converted,*
> *that your sins may be blotted out,*
> *so that times of refreshing may come*
> *from the presence of the Lord."*
> (Acts 3:19 NKJV)

Revival always follows repentance and turning fully back to God.

The Holy Spirit is the breath that revives and empowers. When Jesus breathed on His disciples, He said, "*Receive the Holy Spirit*" (John 20:22 NIV). That same breath brings life to weary souls.

Waiting While Empty

I remember entering prayer desperate to hear or feel God's presence, but there was silence. Shame had engulfed me, and fear outweighed my faith. Still, I kept showing up. I knew He was the only one who could help me. Day after day, I sat in His presence. Sometimes all

I could do was sing, "I don't mind waiting on You, Lord." And I waited.

Slowly, the whispers came. Not condemnation but assurance. He reminded me that He loved me and still desired a relationship with me. He strengthened me with His Word:

He gives strength to the weary
and increases the power of the weak. ...
But those who wait on the LORD
shall renew their strength.
(Isaiah 40:29–31 NKJV)

BREATH IN THE VALLEY

Even as revival began, I kept reminding God of my failures—what I had lost and what I believed I had destroyed. That's when He led me to Ezekiel 37, the valley of dry bones. As I read, the Lord asked me, "Do you believe what looks dead can live again? Do you believe your marriage can live? Do you believe your ministry can live? Do you believe you can live again?" I whispered, "Yes, I believe, but help my unbelief." Then He instructed me to prophesy, not from perfection but from obedience.

Little by little, as I remained in His presence and stayed anchored in His Word, life returned. He replenished me. He promises, "*For I will satisfy the weary soul, and every languishing soul I will replenish*" (Jeremiah 31:25 ESV).

God restored my faith, hope, joy, strength, courage, and passion for ministry. Revival was not sudden. It was intentional, patient, and personal.

THE QUIET WORK OF REVIVAL

Revival and restoration require faith and patience. We often give up because we do not feel immediate change. But it is impossible to enter God's presence without an exchange taking place. Each time we show up, He removes what no longer belongs and deposits what we need. God looks at the heart. Revival does not respond to words alone; it responds to surrender. The heart reveals when repentance is genuine and when faith is present.

Without faith it is impossible to please God.
(Hebrews 11:6 NIV)

THE LINGERING WOUND

Although God revived me, my soul still needed healing. The wound was not fully closed. Macy Catheter explains it this way: A soul injury is a deep, "unassessed wound that separates one from their 'real self' that causes a person to feel personally defective, inadequate, or unworthy."[9] The lingering wound is an unseen injury left behind by trauma. When trauma goes unhealed, it produces prolonged suffering, that shows up as shame, emptiness, emotional numbness, and a loss of meaning. These wounds do not disappear with time; they settle deep within the soul, shaping our thoughts, behaviors, and beliefs long after the pain has diminished. Soul injuries run deep and must by brought to light and healed by God.

This is a process of healing that takes time and intentionality.

I was not dead, but tender. Revived, but not yet whole. Revival restored my breath. But healing would restore my identity. And that is where the next work began.

***

Reflection

What is God showing me?
What did God reveal to me through this chapter?
What area of my heart, thinking, or behavior is He inviting me to bring into alignment?

Biblical Truth to Carry

He gives strength to the weary and increases the power of the weak. ... But those who wait on the LORD shall renew their strength (Isaiah 40:29–31 NKJV).

Closing Prayer

Abba Father,
Thank You for binding every wound and healing every injury. Thank You for helping me to refocus on You and reviving me back to the life You ordained. In the name of Jesus, amen.

Chapter Five: Reinstall

Placed Back into Purpose

To reinstall means to place back into position again.[10] Sometimes we do not leave the path God set for us intentionally. Sometimes pain, exhaustion, fear, or soul injury causes us to step aside. But stepping aside does not mean we are disqualified. God is faithful to restore us to a position when the time is right. I remember clearly the moment I was reinstalled.

I had previously helped a school with marketing materials, and one day the CEO called and invited me to attend their graduation. I told her I would think about it. She insisted gently, saying, "Please come, I really want you there." Truthfully, I had no intention of going. I had been out of circulation a long time. I had withdrawn from people, platforms, and public spaces. The thought of being in a room full of people felt overwhelming. But then the Holy Spirit spoke clearly and simply: "Go."

I immediately responded with resistance. "What am I going to wear?" And just like that, the Holy Spirit answered, telling me what suit to wear, what blouse to put on, and even which shoes to choose. He dressed me for the assignment before I understood the assignment. Though I was not feeling my best emotionally, I obeyed.

Positioned by Obedience

I arrived and took my seat in the audience, quietly observing as people moved about preparing for the graduation ceremony. I had no expectations, only obedience. Then suddenly, the CEO looked out into the crowd and gestured to me, asking me to come forward. I looked around, thinking she must be speaking to someone else. But she gestured to me again. I walked to the front, assuming she might have a question about the marketing materials or needed assistance with something related to the program. Instead, she asked me to take a seat on the platform with the other ministers, doctors, and leaders.

I was stunned. As the ceremony continued, individuals were honored and presented with gifts and awards. Then to my complete surprise, the CEO called my name. This time, she presented me with a gift.

I sat there in shock. And that's when I heard the Holy Spirit say, "Today, you are being reinstalled."

CONFIRMED BY GOD

In that moment, I understood. This was not only an invitation to an event; it was a divine repositioning. God was restoring me, not only to visibility but to community too. He was placing me back among women who would see me, support me, and walk with me. But He was also reinstalling me to a position I thought I had lost forever. I had believed God could never trust me again; however, through this experience, I was forever changed.

I had not asked for a platform. I had not pursued recognition. I had simply obeyed. And obedience led me back into alignment.

Reinstallation is not about promotion; it's about placement.

God says to each of us,

"For I know the plans I have for you,"
declares the LORD,

"plans to prosper you and not to harm you, plans to give you hope and a future."
(Jeremiah 29:11 NIV)

When God reinstalls you, He does it gently, intentionally, and publicly enough to silence the lies of the enemy but privately enough to protect your heart. That day, God reminded me that I was never removed because He could not trust me but because I needed restoration.

Reinstallation is not merely being healed; it is being trusted again. It is not only recovery but also reinstatement into purpose.

Many people experience God's healing yet struggle to step back into the place God originally called them to. Fear, shame, regret, and memory of failure often convince us that what we lost can never be regained. This is exactly how I felt and thought.

But God does not merely restore what is broken; He reinstalls what He ordained. Peter struggled with fear, shame, and regret because he had denied Jesus. He had boldly declared his loyalty to Jesus yet denied Him three times in His darkest hour. Overcome by fear, shame, and regret, Peter wept bitterly (Matthew 26:33–35, 69–75). In his mind, his failure disqualified him forever. Yet after the resurrection, Jesus did not confront Peter publicly, shame him, or dismiss him. Instead. He restored him privately and then reinstalled him intentionally.

In John 21, Jesus met Peter by the sea and asked him three times: *"Do you love Me?"* Each question gently restored the relationship and healed a denial. Each response rebuilt trust and reactivated the divine loyalty Peter felt toward Jesus. And then Jesus gave Peter his assignment back: *"Feed My sheep."* With those words, Peter was not only forgiven but he was also recommissioned. Jesus did not remove Peter from leadership. He returned him to it. Peter emerged more humble, more dependent, and more powerful. Shortly after, Peter stepped out boldly and preached the greatest sermon ever, and over three thousand souls were saved (Acts 2). God reinstalled him into leadership, influence, and impact.

Like Peter, I was feeling fear, shame, and regret, but I remember the day Abba Father said to me in a still, small voice, "I still want you to teach My Word."

Through this experience, I learned that denial does not disqualify you, and failure does not cancel calling.

I had been revived. I had been refined. Now I was reinstalled. But reinstatement was not the end of the journey. God was preparing to reset, renew, and realign me fully—mind, heart, and identity. And the restoration continues.

*****

REFLECTION

What is God showing me?
What did God reveal to me through this chapter?
What area of my heart, thinking, or behavior is He inviting me to bring into alignment?

BIBLICAL TRUTH TO CARRY

"*For I know the plans I have for you,*" *declares the* L*ORD*, "*plans to prosper you and not to harm you, plans to give you hope and a future*" (Jeremiah 29:11 NIV).

CLOSING PRAYER

Abba Father,
Thank You for revealing to me that Your gifts are irrevocable and nothing I do can permanently terminate me from the call on my life. Thank You for delivering me from shame and guilt and helping me to trust myself again. In the name of Jesus, amen.

Chapter Six: Reset

Divine Interruption

Reset is defined as "returning to an original position, to set again after disruption."[11]

After revival and reinstatement, I realized that restoration alone was not enough. God had revived my spirit and reinstalled me into community; but patterns, pace, and posture still needed attention. I needed to be reset before I could get back out there to conduct ministry. I could not move forward carrying the same survival habits that had nearly destroyed me into a new season of purpose.

At some point in my journey, joining a religion and adopting its perspectives caused me to lose myself. I lost myself in striving and trying to earn the love of God to the extent that I forgot who Shannon was. I forgot that my entire life had already been orchestrated by God: the visions, dreams, successes, failures, losses, and victories. Even before I consciously knew Him, He knew me, guided me, and covered me. I forgot the people I poured into and the evidence of His hand that had always been with me.

As a little girl, I spoke to grown women, and they said, “How do you know these things? You have so much wisdom. I should be telling you, but you are helping me.” My peers joked that I acted like an old lady. But it was not age; it was the Spirit of wisdom speaking through me. The Holy Spirit guided me like a cloud over my head, giving me insight, discernment, and wisdom far beyond my years.

God’s hand was always on my life. Somehow, my needs were met even when I had very little. As a young mother, He gave me the wisdom and strength to raise four beautiful children. He protected me in moments when danger surrounded me. On several occasions, I heard Him whisper, “Leave now,” and shortly after, violence broke out. I endured physical, mental, and emotional abuse. I was beaten with a baseball bat and struck in the head with a gun. All of it was meant for my destruction, yet God preserved me.

So the question became: How did I end up broken if God had always been with me?

The answer was identity, faith, and grace.

I got caught up in religion.

Religion teaches knowledge about God but does not anchor identity in Him. It emphasizes works over grace, performance over relationship, and striving over trust. Over time, constant exposure to judgment and performance-based theology caused me to forget who I was in Christ. I began working for a righteousness I already possessed and striving for a grace that had already been given. 2 Corinthians 5:21 says,

God made [Christ], who had no sin,
to be sin for us, so that in him
we might become the righteousness of God. (NIV)

I had forgotten that God chose me, saved me, and adopted me—not because I was perfect but because I answered when He called and humbled myself before Him.

Abba Father had to reset me by reconnecting me to my true identity. He led me to Ephesians chapters 1 and 2 and asked me to read them again with fresh eyes.

Through those scriptures, He reminded me:

- I am blessed.
- I am chosen.
- I am adopted.
- I am righteous.
- I am a child of God.
- I am accepted.
- I am redeemed.
- I am forgiven.
- I am sealed with the Holy Spirit of promise.
- I am resurrected.
- I am saved.

Reset required a process of elimination—removing false beliefs, distorted theology, and identities shaped by fear, then replacing them with revelational truth to strengthen and heal what remained. I had to remove what was false before I could fully receive what was true.

When God Interrupted My Patterns

For years, I lived on overdrive. I stayed busy to avoid feeling. I stayed productive to feel valuable. I stayed available to feel accepted. Even after healing began, those old survival patterns tried to follow me into my new season. God, in His mercy, interrupted me.

Reset required me to slow down long enough to notice what was misaligned. It forced me to confront habits that looked spiritual on the outside but were draining me on the inside. I had to admit that I did not know how to rest properly. I did not think clearly or respond wisely because I had lived in crisis mode for so long. The reset was not punishment; it was protection. God must peel off the layer of religion to get to the core of who we truly are to reset us.

What God Began to Reset

During this season, the Father began resetting areas I didn't even realize were damaged:

- My thinking: replacing fear-based thoughts with truth
- My pace: teaching me that urgency is not obedience

- My boundaries: showing me that access must be earned not assumed
- My yes and no: restoring discernment
- My identity: separating who I am from what I do

I learned that if I did not allow God to reset me, I would repeat cycles He had already delivered me from.

Rest: The Sacred Companion of Reset

Rest became an essential part of my reset. Without ministry demands and constant church activity, God created space for me to rest mentally, physically, spiritually, and most importantly, in my soul.

At first, rest felt uncomfortable. I even felt guilty for not spending hours studying my Bible the way I once had. But Abba Father gently whispered, "It's okay." He was teaching me to rest in His presence, not strive for it.

God exchanged my yoke for His. The weight of performance and pressure was replaced with a yoke that was easy and light. I watched romantic comedies and

Christmas movies without condemnation, all while sensing Him say, “I’m still with you.”

There were nights my body awakened me to pray out of habit, and again I heard Him say, “Shannon, just rest.”

God never called us to be busy bodies. Even He rested on the seventh day. Jesus withdrew after ministry to rest and be restored. Rest is not laziness or complacency; it is trust.

The Hard Truth About Reset

Reset feels uncomfortable because it removes familiarity. Familiar chaos can feel safer than unfamiliar peace.

But God does not reset us to confuse us; He resets us to prepare us. In Isaiah 43:18–19, God says,

“Forget the former things; do not dwell on the past.
See, I am doing a new thing! Now it springs up;
do you not perceive it?” (NIV)

Reset positioned me to perceive what God was doing instead of reacting to what I had been through.

God did not reset me to erase my past. He reset me to realign my identity. And once identity is restored, everything else can follow. Alignment with your identity changes you forever; everything you think, do, or say comes from the revelation of knowing who you are and whose you are.

*****

REFLECTION

What is God showing me?
What did God reveal to me through this chapter?
What area of my heart, thinking, or behavior is He inviting me to bring into alignment?

BIBLICAL TRUTH TO CARRY

God made [Christ], who had no sin to be sin for us, so that in him we might become the righteousness of God (2 Corinthians 5:21 NIV).

Closing Prayer

Abba Father,

Thank You for teaching me to rest in You and release unhealthy patterns. In the name of Jesus, amen.

CHAPTER SEVEN: RENEW

INNER TRANSFORMATION

To renew means to begin again or to be restored with increased strength.[12]

Renewal begins in the mind. It reshapes thought patterns and transforms beliefs. If I learned anything through this experience, it was this: Falling does not always mean failure. For a long time, I believed I had failed as a servant, a leader, and a disciple. I convinced myself I had disqualified my calling and forfeited God's use of my life, which made me lose desire for ministry. I no longer wanted to attend church because every message seemed to confirm the hopeless narrative playing in my mind.

Yet what was happening internally did not align with what I was feeling externally. My mind told me it was over. My body was breaking down under pain, illness, and exhaustion. But my spirit was being renewed day by day. I was not falling from grace; I was falling back into grace. I was not falling out of the will of God; I was being realigned with it. I was falling out of religion and back into a relationship. God was renewing me, and the proof was His peace.

Renewed, Not Rejected

God began dismantling religious strongholds and renewing my mind. While condemning thoughts bombarded me, He gently invited me to let the mind of Christ dwell in me. Jesus never looked to religious leaders for approval or coverage. He looked only to the Father. He knew He was already accepted, already provided for, already covered. Every decision He made flowed from His relationship with the Father. We see this in His actions. Whatever decision He faced, whatever He needed, He looked to the Father. He fed me with His daily bread to nourish me and renew my mind.

That revelation transformed me.

Our minds are renewed through faith, and *faith comes by hearing, and hearing by the word of God* (Romans 10:17 NKJV). God positioned me to hear His Word alone—not opinions, not condemnation, not performance-based theology—so He could rebuild my faith correctly. Peace became my anchor.

Abba Father's peace is always an indicator of alignment, even when everything around you is falling apart. One morning, God led me to the story of Elijah in 1 Kings 19. Elijah was a powerful prophet who had just witnessed God move mightily, yet one threat from Jezebel sent him running to hide in fear. Overwhelmed, exhausted, depressed, discouraged, and suicidal, Elijah hid in a cave and cried out to God. In his despair, he confessed that he was no better than his ancestors and asked God to take his life.

But God did not shame Elijah for his fear or dismiss him for being discouraged. Instead, God met him in his weakness. He allowed Elijah to rest while providing daily nourishment. Then He spoke to Elijah—not through the wind, earthquake, or fire but in a still, small voice. The enemy uses the wind, earthquakes, and fire to instill fear into the believer, but God always speaks in a soft, gentle, loving voice.

When God asked Elijah, *"What are you doing here?"* it was not a question of condemnation but of restoration (1 Kings 19:13). Though Elijah felt defeated and discouraged, God reminded him that he was not alone and that his assignment was not finished. Rather than releasing Elijah from service, God renewed him and sent him back to ministry with purpose. He instructed Elijah to anoint three individuals, signaling that Elijah's calling still stood. Fear, fatigue, and self-pity had not disqualified him. God restored Elijah and recommissioned him.

Renewal did not remove Elijah's humanity; it restored his strength and reminded him of his identity and purpose. Through this story, God revealed the confirmation of His still, small voice when He said to me, "I still want you to teach My Word." I thought I was not ready to return to ministry. He showed me through this scripture that restoration continues through your ordained assignment as we go to serve in ministry.

People often ask how I could lose so much health, community, and confidence yet still remain at peace. The answer is simple: God is peace. His peace surpasses understanding and sustains us while renewal is taking place. Understanding the revelation of peace during a storm is an indication of God's presence, which changed my perspective so I could see my situation from God's point of view.

His peace dismantled thought patterns that told me:

- God was finished with me.
- I had disqualified myself.
- I was no longer loved or accepted.

Even while my life looked shattered, God placed His peace within me to remind me that His love was not based on my behavior but on His nature.

GRACE RECLAIMED

Thank God, everything was stripped away except my love for prayer and His presence so that He could dismantle religious thinking at the root. He renewed my faith to receive the gift of grace.

For it is by grace you have been saved, through faith—and this is not from yourselves, it is the gift of God.
(Ephesians 2:8 NIV)

One day in prayer, God asked me, "Shannon, do you pay for the gifts you receive on your birthday?"

I replied, "No."

He said, "Neither do you pay for the gift I gave you. Jesus paid for it. I'm simply giving it to you."

That revelation shattered years of performance-driven belief. Confidence rushed in like rivers of living water.

This is the confidence I now live by: The work God started in me, He will finish. While He continues His work, I have full permission to dwell boldly in His kingdom, preach His Word, and walk in purpose.

I am qualified because He qualifies.

I am called because He calls.

I am appointed for such a time as this, and no one can revoke what God has ordained.

Renewal That Reaches the Body

As my mind was renewed, hidden thought patterns surfaced that had contributed to stress, anxiety, and even physical illness. God allowed them to rise because they did not belong to me.

Through the apostle John, God says,

"Beloved, I pray that you may prosper in all things and be in health, just as your soul prospers."
(3 John 1:2 NKJV)

He is the Potter. I am the clay. He brings what is hidden to the surface so He can remove it. Trauma teaches us to hide scars or pretend pain never happened. But God wastes nothing. He gathers broken pieces and restores them in a way that makes us more beautiful than before.

BEAUTY IN BROKENNESS

This process reminds me of *kintsugi*, a Japanese art form that repairs broken pottery with gold. Instead of hiding the cracks, gold is used to highlight them, creating a piece that is stronger, more functional, and more valuable than before.

This is how God renews us.

He does not erase the breaks; He redeems them.

He takes the mess and makes it a message.
He turns trials into testimony.

He transforms wounds into authentic worship.

THE TIME IT TAKES TO RENEW

Renewal takes time.

Just as kintsugi requires patience, sometimes months for the process to complete, God takes His time with us. I was in no rush to return to ministry. I wanted God to remove every impurity so that when He released me, I would function with integrity, humility, and Christlike character.

Renewal must happen in the mind, spirit, and belief system.

Though betrayal and loss damaged my confidence and left me feeling empty, I never stopped feeding on the Word. God's Word was my daily bread. Without it, I knew I would become spiritually malnourished. So, I asked God to give me revelation through His daily bread, and I ate of it as I waited.

But they that wait upon the L*ORD*
shall renew their strength.
(Isaiah 40:31 KJV)

I waited even when I did not fully understand what I was waiting for. I learned that transformation is not always visible during the process. It is revealed in the outcome. Day by day, the process showed that God was renewing my belief in a way that it would never be shaken again.

FROM RELIGIOUS BELIEF TO DIVINE REVELATION

There is a difference between religious belief and divine belief. Religious belief is based on what you see; so, when the structure collapses, belief collapses with it. Revelational belief is birthed by the Holy Spirit. It becomes an internalized truth that cannot be shaken.

One day, while comparing myself to others, the Holy Spirit spoke to me: "Shannon, all you have to do is be and become."

I finally understood that I was already knitted together with everything I needed. I did not need to become someone else. I simply needed to exist as God created me to be.

I was never incomplete. I was complete in Him.

I did not need to replace myself. I needed renewal in my thinking.

*****

Reflection

What is God showing me?
What did God reveal to me through this chapter?
What area of my heart, thinking, or behavior is He inviting me to bring into alignment?

Biblical Truth to Carry

But they that wait upon the LORD shall renew their strength (Isaiah 40:31 KJV).

Closing Prayer

Abba Father,
Thank You for reminding me that all things are possible through You. Thank You for showing me that I am not rejected. I am renewed in You. You are an eternal refreshment; Your rivers never stop running. Thank You for restoring me stronger, more functional, and more valuable than before. In the name of Jesus, amen.

Chapter Eight: Reclaiming my Authority

Taking Back What Was Lost

To reclaim means to take back what already belonged to you.[13]

After betrayal, loss, and spiritual warfare, I found myself wounded and stunned—so overwhelmed that I became silent. Without realizing it, I had surrendered my authority and allowed the enemy to take territory that was never his to possess.

This is how the enemy operates.

Just as he did in the garden of Eden, he does not begin by attacking our body; he begins by attacking our beliefs. He plants doubt, distorts truth, and pressures us into silence. His goal is not only to hurt us but also to mute us, because he knows we have power in our voice.

Jesus made this clear when He said,

"Whoever says to this mountain,
'Be removed and be cast into the sea,'
and does not doubt in his heart, but believes that
those things he says will be done,
he will have whatever he says."
(Mark 11:23 NKJV)

What we speak in faith carries authority. When we speak what God's Word has already established, heaven responds. Silence, however, is costly. God gave Adam authority and dominion in the garden, and Adam surrendered it to the enemy. The serpent gave the woman the fruit; then she gave it to Adam, who remained silent and ate it. Had he spoken up in authority and refused to eat the fruit, the test in the garden would have turned out differently.

Responding to the enemy by speaking the word in authority is a sign that you stand in your dominion. Jesus stood in dominion when He was tested in the wilderness (Matthew 4). Once the enemy silences you, he has gained ground—not because he has power over you but because authority was yielded. Another strategy of the enemy is to steal praise, because praise is a weapon.

THE POWER OF PRAISE AND THE RECOVERY

God once showed me a vision of a multitude of unclean spirits gathered. He simply said one word to me: "Praise." I began to shout "hallelujah" over and over. With each declaration, the spirits scattered. I continued until they were completely gone.

Then I saw something else—gifts bound tightly with ropes. God revealed to me that these were the things the enemy had stolen from me. That day, I received a revelation: Praise is a weapon. It confuses the enemy and dismantles his plans. Praise invites God to intervene as Judge and Defender.

God also let me know that when we pray and praise, the enemy loses territory, but in the times we do not, he regains territory. I learned that daily prayer and praise are not optional; they are essential.

AUTHORITY RESTORED

The enemy himself has no authority over believers. He cannot destroy your life unless permission is granted. We see this clearly in the story of Job:

> *Now there was a day when the sons of God came to present themselves before the* L*ORD, and Satan also came among them.* (Job 1:6–7 ESV)

Satan appeared before God, accusing Job of serving Him only to receive blessings and possessions. He claimed that Job's righteousness was not authentic, that if God stretched out His hand and touched all Job had, he would curse Him. God permitted Satan to touch Job's possessions but not his life. Satan could only act within boundaries set by God.

Satan roams the earth looking for legal access, seeking those who step outside of God's covering through fear, ignorance, or disobedience. Many believers forfeit God's promises—not because God withholds them but because of a lack of alignment with truth. God warns us: *"My people are destroyed for lack of knowledge"* (Hosea 4:6 NKJV). However, God is a restorer.

What Is Forfeited Can Be Reclaimed

God is a restorer; however, some things are forfeited, not stolen, because rules were broken or wisdom was ignored. God's Word is the blueprint for victorious living.

God told Joshua:

"Keep this Book of the Law always on your lips;
meditate on it day and night,
so that you may be careful
to do everything written in it.
Then you will be prosperous and successful."
(Joshua 1:8 NIV)

Success and prosperity are tied to knowledge, meditation, and obedience.

When God revealed this to me, I said, "I repent for my ignorance."

He replied, "Ignorance does not exempt you from consequence."

Why? Because His Word contains everything that pertains to life and righteous living. But it must be pursued, learned, and applied.

One of the enemy's greatest strategies in this generation is distraction. We live in an age of information overload, yet spiritual ignorance persists. Knowledge alone does not produce fruit; the knowledge of God does. We are to study to show ourselves approved and apply God's Word to daily living (2 Timothy 2:15). Disobedience often stems from unlearned truth. Fear and distractions keep us from obeying. Doubt paralyzes movement. But reclamation begins when responsibility is owned, and revelation is received.

One morning, in my devotional time with God. I was praying for my children. All of a sudden, my two arms lifted and stretched out. God demonstrated to me that I was covering them, my arms as a shield, and over me, where the arms of God sheltered me. This vision ignited my authority to the next level.

He led me to the word in 2 Chronicles 20:21–22: *Praise the LORD, for His mercy endures forever.* When the people *began to sing and to praise, the LORD set up ambushes* against their enemy, and they were defeated (NKJV). I knew this was my opportunity to reclaim all that was taken from me.

I went into intercession with confidence, knowing the LORD was shielding me. I repented for any transgressions that gave the enemy legal ground. I declared my authority given by Jesus, and I reclaimed all that belongs to me, my children, and grandchildren—canceling out attacks and reclaiming territory and God's divine order and promises for my marriage, ministry, and my life. I declared and saturated the Word of God over my children and grandchildren, breaking generational curses, mindsets, belief systems, and strongholds influenced by the enemy. I declared we live in God divine blessings, destiny and purpose as righteous children.

RELIGION VS. REVELATION

This is why God detests religion. Religion creates its own systems, replaces revelation with routine, and follows man's methods instead of God's truth. Jesus said, *"I am the way, the truth, and the life"* (John 14:6 NKJV).

He is the Word. When we follow the Word, we prevent the enemy from robbing us. When we equip ourselves with the Word, we move with authority to reclaim what the enemy has stolen.

We lose ground when:

- We do not study the Word.
- We walk in disobedience.

- We walk in fear.
- We resist correction.

But what is forfeited can be restored.

My Declaration of Reclamation

I repented and asked God to cleanse my inheritance and restore what had been forfeited.

I reclaimed:

- My authority
- My voice
- My territory
- My possessions
- My confidence
- My boldness

In the name of Jesus, I declared a double portion.

Today, I no longer shrink back. I stand boldly in the authority God has given me. He has restored my courage to speak without fear of rejection or retaliation.

I have taken back my territory
in my home,
in my ministry,
and in my personal life.

What the enemy tried to silence, God has amplified.

What was surrendered has been reclaimed.

What was lost has been restored.

*****

REFLECTION

What is God showing me?
What did God reveal to me through this chapter?
What area of my heart, thinking, or behavior is He inviting me to bring into alignment?

BIBLICAL TRUTH TO CARRY

God said, "*Keep this Book of the Law always on your lips; meditate on it day and night, so that you may be careful to do everything written in it. Then you will be prosperous and successful*" (Joshua 1:8 NIV).

Closing Prayer

Abba Father,

Thank You for restoring my voice, authority, and identity in You. Thank You for delivering me from religion and realigning me with revelation. In the name of Jesus, amen.

Chapter Nine: Realigned

Getting Back in Order

Realignment is the act or instance of restoring or changing to a previous or different position. It is organized or arranged in a new way. Through my process, I was uncertain, numb, angry, and afraid because I did not understand what was happening. Today I know that everything I went through was for realignment. As we embark on our journey and life unfolds, we can be pushed out of alignment with God and His purpose for our lives. If we are not in the proper position in our relationship with God, the misalignment can take us totally off course.

At one time, I had an old vehicle. Without warning, the steering wheel sometimes shook, and the car pulled to one side. When I took it to the mechanic, he said the car needed a wheel alignment. I once read a blog post on what happens when you drive a car with bad wheel alignment. The writer explained what makes a vehicle drive properly: "A car's steering and suspension system connects the body of your car to the wheels that propel it forward. So, when the alignment is off, it can throw your whole vehicle out of sync."[14] Driving a vehicle with a bad alignment not only causes the steering wheel to shake and the car to veer toward the side, but it also wears down your tires prematurely.

When we are out of alignment with God, it shakes us to the core of our souls, pulling us off the path of purpose and destiny. There is a reason the Word of God warns us not to look to the left or right, but to look up. Looking up to the Father is what keeps us on the right path, but being in perfect alignment with the Father gives us the strength and endurance to journey with divine purpose and destiny. Just as a bad wheel alignment throws the car out of sync, so it is with God's children when we are out of alignment with Him.

When we are out of sync with the Father, it wears us down prematurely. Just as a mechanic uses specialized equipment to adjust a car's suspension system, God uses trials and tribulations to adjust and realign us with His plan and purpose. I thought my trials and tribulations were pushing me further from God, but instead they were pulling me into His presence. The more I went through, the more I cried out to the Father, even if it was

to ask "Why?" to get an understanding or "How?" to help get back on the path of righteousness.
In Jeremiah 32:39, God declares,

> *"I will give them one heart and one way,*
> *that they may fear Me forever,*
> *for the good of them and their children."* (NKJV)

This reveals God's desire for His children to live with one heart, one purpose, and one direction toward Him. He longs for us to be in perfect alignment with His will because alignment is how we gain access to His promises and protection.

Alignment, however, requires surrender. Jesus makes this clear in Mark 8:34: "*Whoever desires to come after Me, let him deny himself, and take up his cross and follow Me*" (NKJV). Realignment always begins with self-denial, which means we cannot hold on to control, comfort, or our agenda. To realign means to let go of who we think we should be and submit to who God has called us to become.

The Bible shows us how the children of Israel struggled with aligning themselves with God, because they could not fully release their past. No matter how God showed up for them, they refused to let go of old mindsets, pride, and idolatry. Because of this, they repeatedly fell out of step with God's direction. The problem with being out of alignment with God is that we can never carry out God's divine purpose for our lives nor receive the benefits and promises He wants to release to us. The generation that left Egypt never experienced what God had in store for them.

Realignment is not about reconnecting with past seasons, identities, or familiar patterns. It is about embracing the new thing God wants to do in our life. The children of Israel kept going in circles because they were trying to follow the image in their mind of how things should be rather than fully relying on God to lead them where He had assigned them to be.

I also struggled with letting go of my past and the image I had in my mind of how God would use me in ministry. I realized in the secret place that I had to fully submit and trust God's plan and purpose, even if I did not know what it was. Submission and trusting in God is about going by faith without knowledge of the full plan. I realized I needed to adopt an Abrahamic mindset. When God told Abraham to leave his country and family, he departed as God spoke to him, immediately showing faith in God.

SUBMISSION

To realign with God, it takes full submission.

It is God who works in you
both to will and to do for His good pleasure.
(Philippians 2:13 NKJV)

Furthermore, He tells us to submit our way to Him, and He will give us the desire of our heart. When we submit our way to God, He aligns our desires with His will. What once felt unclear becomes crystal clear. What was once forced begins to flow.

"How do I get back into alignment with You, Abba Father?" I asked God that question, not knowing I would be forever changed by the answer. I began to lose the desire to go to church. I was so turned off, and I could not understand why, because I have always loved going into the church building. It was my life, and now I was losing love for what I loved doing the most.

Little by little, I let go. I let go of my ministry, stopped preaching on Sundays and Thursdays. I shut down the prayer line and only prayed in the morning with one faithful member who insisted on staying and praying with me. God met us in the morning, and I received a daily dose of strength and peace. I thank God for that prayer partner every day. She is a rare servant of the Lord who serves so selflessly.

During this time, I sat down, read my Bible, then sat some more. All I wanted to do was sit quietly in the presence of God. I did not know Him that well as Abba Father, but I knew I always found comfort in His presence. I had no words to speak because I was numb, or maybe in shock, because I thought church was the way, truth, and life I ought to live forever. I made an oath to dwell in the house of the Lord forever, and now I felt like forever was coming to an end.

Thoughts bombarded my mind. If I do not have God, who am I? How do I exist without Him? In those questions, I discovered that I subconsciously used the church body to define me. At some point, I intertwined God and the church building, and that was costing me my faith, identity, and peace, so I left the church building.

WHY DID I LEAVE THE CHURCH?

I left the church to realign with God and reconnect with my identity and faith. Today's church focuses on emotions, status, and characteristics. It has become about who is liked and who is not liked. Who has status and popularity, and who does not. Too often, churches focus on the bad characteristics of a person rather than the restoration of the person's soul.

God desires that all His children prosper and be in good health. One thing we know to be true is that whatever we focus on the most becomes a mountain in our life, and that thing consumes us. Therefore, focusing on the bad characteristics of a person only draws out more of the bad. However, proclaiming and explaining the good characteristics enlightens the person, renews the mind, and transforms the life. It is Satan's desire to illuminate the incomplete characteristics of a person to condemn them, because he intends to sift them as wheat (Luke 22:31).

The Father intends that we learn, grow, and evolve into the complete characteristics of Christ. Though we expect children to behave in a certain manner, we must remember that transformation takes time. The Word says, *Just as your soul prospers*. The word *prosper* suggests a process of time. Restoration and transformation are never completed in one day. Anything that loses its original identity, function, or value must go through the process of restoration. This entails an investigation to determine the cause of the malfunction and examine the damage, then the process to restore it to its original purpose.

This can only be done by God our Creator, not by the church body. Therefore, God had to take me on a journey of restoration and reconnect me with my true identity in private. Leaving the church exposed what had been wounded in me, but it also revealed what had become misaligned. While I had distanced myself from systems, I realized my soul still needed to be reordered by God Himself. Healing could not begin externally; it had to begin internally. Before restoration could happen, alignment had to be restored.

ALIGN MY SOUL

As I cried out to God, "I am desperate for You, Lord," I prayed that He would realign my soul. Scripture tells us, the LORD God *breathed into his [Adam's] nostrils the breath of life, and the man became a living being.*

(Genesis 2:7 NIV). I needed my soul to live and thrive again from God's divine source of life.

One prayer I consistently pray over my life is from 3 John 1:2. I pray that I will prosper in all things and be in health, just as my soul prospers. Yet I now understand that true prosperity and health cannot exist unless the soul first prospers through God's divine intervention.

The soul is the seat of our consciousness, but God must be the One who occupies the seat. He is the source of life that allows the soul to live, and He must be the substance that fills it in order for it to thrive. Whenever we are out of alignment with God, the soul begins to suffer and decline. When this happens, our identity, character, and dispositions are affected, along with our mind, memory, and imagination.

Thank God for the Holy Spirit, who advocates for us and reminds us of everything the Lord has spoken concerning us. He quickens our spirit and draws us back into alignment, compelling us to cry out to the Father once again.

A Realignment Prayer

"Abba Father, I ask that You will breathe upon me and realign my soul with Your breath. Align my thoughts with Your thoughts. Align my heart with Your heart so that when You look upon me, You will see a woman after Your own heart. Let my soul thrive and live according to Your original design and purpose for my life. Cleanse my soul from all unrighteousness—every evil thought, influence, suggestion, and stronghold that would cause me to think out of alignment with Your Word. Purge my soul from every thought that exalts itself against the knowledge of You. Restore my soul to the original intent, realigned with the plan and purpose You have established for my life."

Once the soul is realigned, it must be maintained through intimacy. We must remain positioned before God. This is where the secret place becomes essential. The secret place is not an escape from life; it is the place where life is reordered, where the voice of God grows clearer, and where the soul learns to abide rather than strive. God does not just want to realign us. He invites us into a deeper dwelling, where communion eliminates confusion and intimacy becomes the anchor that keeps the soul aligned.

THE SECRET PLACE

Scripture tells us, *He who dwells in the secret place of the Most High shall abide under the shadow of the Almighty* (Psalm 91:1 NKJV). The secret place is not a physical location but a spiritual posture of dwelling with God. It is the place of union with God, where the soul learns to rest, listen, and remain. Here, God does not merely speak to correct us; He speaks to commune with us. In the secret place, distractions lose their voice, wounds are tended, and alignment is sustained through relationship. This is where the soul is reshaped by His truth.

> *He restores my soul; He leads me in the paths of righteousness for His name's sake.*
> (Psalm 23:3 NKJV)

I spent days sitting quietly in the presence of God, not able to utter a word, thinking I was totally disconnected from God. But I discovered I was only disconnected from the church and had been led to the secret place of God. I said, "God, I have said enough. I have no words, so I will just come and sit." But the truth is, I did not need any words; I only needed to sit in His presence and be fully present in the moment for whenever He wanted to speak or reveal something.

Prayer is not about regurgitating all your emotions and thoughts; sometimes it is being fully present in His presence. Prayer is an all-inclusive fellowship with God—being in full awareness, listening, receiving, offering, surrendering, agreeing, exchanging, praising, worshiping, and responding to Him in humility. These are the conduits that help us to realign with Abba Father. This is where correction is made, and growth happens in the dark, quiet place with only God and you. In the secret place, you get realigned and rediscover your identity. In the secret place, you get cleansed from worldly aspirations and refilled with the Holy Spirit of promise.

One morning in prayer, I was led to Acts 4:29–30, where Peter prayed,

> *"Grant to Your servants that with all boldness*
> *they may speak Your word,*
> *by stretching out Your hand to heal,*
> *and that signs and wonders*
> *may be done through the name*
> *of Your holy Servant Jesus."* (NKJV)

God had delivered me from fear, reconnected me with identity and authority, but I needed boldness for the relaunch. This revelation led me to Acts 2:4:

And they were all filled with the Holy Spirit
and began to speak with other tongues,
as the Spirit gave them utterance. (NKJV)

Restoration is not about restoring what was lost; rather, it is about restoring someone to their original condition. The only way to be restored to a divine language is through the filling of the Holy Spirit. That revelation provoked me to cry out, "Abba Father, refill me, refill me and give me utterance to speak Your word boldly that You may stretch out Your hand to heal and deliver Your people and that signs and wonders may be done. Refill me, oh Lord!"

Later that morning, at 6:00 a.m., the mother of my ministry called. She prayed, then I prayed. My prayer in its entirety was filled with only the Word of God. In the end, she said, "Wow! Pastor, it is good to hear you pray with such confidence again."

At her words, I realized God had given me utterance as I had asked, and I had been refilled and restored to divine language—in agreement with a Word that never returns void. This revelational experience gave me the boldness to speak openly and confidently, knowing my words are guided by the Holy Spirit. If He speaks through me, I dwell in this change that lasts forever, and others will be changed by the words I speak.

*****

Reflection

What is God showing me?
What did God reveal to me through this chapter?
What area of my heart, thinking, or behavior is He inviting me to bring into alignment?

Biblical Truth to Carry

God declares, *"I will give them one heart and one way, that they may fear Me forever for the good of them and their children"* (Jeremiah 32:39 NKJV).

Closing Prayer

Abba Father,
Thank You for drawing me into Your secret place and restoring my soul. Teach me how to abide in You and trust You to cover me in the shadow of Your wings. I

surrender every burden, every question, and every unmet expectation at Your feet. Reshape me and restore what was worn and strengthen what has been weak. Order my steps and reposition my heart according to Your purpose. I submit to Your communion and guidance to live from this place. In the name of Jesus, amen.

Chapter Ten: Restored

Living Whole

To restore means to return something or someone to an earlier good condition or rightful position.[15] But restoration in God is never about returning to who you were; it is about revealing who you were always meant to be.

Being out of alignment with God is costly. When alignment is lost, we lose access—not to God Himself but to the benefits that flow from obedience and intimacy with Him. Favor, clarity, peace, honor, authority, and access to divine connections begin to wither when alignment is compromised. As my story reveals, I experienced great loss—not because God abandoned me, but because misalignment separated us.

Yet once I returned to the Father, restoration followed. For a while, I believed I had forfeited the blessings of God, that my mistakes had permanently disqualified me, and that God was finished with me. But through revelation in Ephesians 1, the Holy Spirit corrected my understanding. I learned that spiritual blessings are eternal and irrevocable, and we cannot forfeit them. They exist in heavenly places, they are given by the Father, and they are secured in Christ.

EVERY SPIRITUAL BLESSING REMAINS IN PLACE

When we accept Jesus as Lord and Savior, we receive the Holy Spirit and are sealed as our eternal inheritance. He dwells with us forever. Mercy is renewed daily. Grace remains sufficient. Salvation is secure. The blood of Jesus covers us even in seasons when we are out of touch or misaligned. These spiritual blessings operate continually—keeping us, sustaining us, and preserving us.

What we truly lose access to is not spiritual inheritance but earthly blessings—the tangible rewards of obedience, stewardship, and alignment. These are the things Scripture warns us not to idolize, because they can be shaken, removed, or stolen.

As Jesus reminds us in Matthew 6:19:

> *"Do not store up for yourselves treasures on earth,*
> *where moths and vermin destroy,*
> *and where thieves break in and steal."* (NIV)

Scripture gives us powerful examples of restoration following repentance and realignment. King Nebuchadnezzar is the main character in the greatest story of restoration ever told. King Nebuchadnezzar, once a mighty ruler, allowed pride to corrupt his heart. Though God warned him, he failed to submit until everything was stripped away. But when he lifted his eyes to heaven, repented, and acknowledged the sovereignty of the Most High God, his understanding returned. Glory, honor, and authority were restored, and greater majesty was added (Daniel 4).

The same is true in the life of Job. After losing health, wealth, family, and relationships, God restored him and then gave him double for his trouble (Job 42). God does not merely replace what was lost; He restores with increase.

And the same is true for me. After repentance and realignment, God began to restore all favor, clarity, peace, honor, authority, and access to divine connections. He restored my marriage, ministry, divine relationships, and most importantly, my love and passion for Him and His kingdom and His people.

This is the nature of divine restoration.

HOW RESTORATION CHANGED HOW I APPROACH MINISTRY

Restoration did not return me to the ministry I once knew; it redefined how I serve entirely.

Before, I ministered from obligation, performance, and identity entanglement. I measured fruit by visibility, effectiveness by activity, and faithfulness by endurance. I believed being constantly available meant being obedient. I confused productivity with purpose and sacrifice with surrender.

Now, I approach ministry from alignment, intimacy, and obedience.

I no longer serve to be seen; I serve from being sent.
I no longer move out of urgency; I move with intentionality by discernment.

I no longer carry what God never assigned me to hold.

Ministry is no longer my identity; it is an overflow of it. I have learned that access must be qualified not assumed. Rest is not optional; it is obedience. Silence is not absence; it is often instruction. And fruitfulness does not come from striving but from abiding.

I now understand that when ministry costs you your soul, it is no longer ministry; it is misalignment.

God restored my authority by first restoring my alignment. He restored my voice by grounding it in truth not trauma. He restored my calling by anchoring it in relationship not reputation.

Restoration is the evidence of a life fully aligned with God. It is acknowledging His divine dominion and understanding that my existence is part of something far greater than myself. It is knowing that my identity is rooted in Him—not in titles, platforms, or roles.

Restoration is yielding fully to the Holy Spirit and trusting Him as my life's GPS. Outside of Him, I am undone. But connected to Him, I am complete, anchored, and prosperous.

It is choosing to walk by faith rather than sight. To seek wisdom daily and allow wisdom to have her way. To confess that my gifts, skills, and success are not my own; they are entrusted to me for the glory of God.
What God has done in restoring my life is the greatest experience I will ever know. There is no joy greater than reconnection to divine identity. To know that God formed me, covers me, and thinks precious thoughts toward me. To understand that I am not hidden from God but hidden in Him.

I am fearfully and wonderfully made. My story was written in perfection by God before I ever lived a single chapter. I embrace my story in its entirety—the good, bad, and indifferent—with honor and gladness, because I now understand that every chapter works for my good and brings Him glory. And God's desire for me to prosper, to be whole, and to be healthy in body, mind, and soul has always remained unchanged.

*****

Reflection

What is God showing me?

What did God reveal to me through this chapter?

What area of my heart, thinking, or behavior is He inviting me to bring into alignment?

Biblical Truth to Carry

Jesus said, *"Do not store up for yourselves treasures on earth, where moths and vermin destroy, and where thieves break in and steal"* (Matthew 6:19 NIV).

Closing Prayer

Abba Father,
Thank You for helping me to live whole, secure, and submitted to Your Spirit. In the name of Jesus, amen.

CONCLUSION:

HOW I NOW SEE REJECTION

REJECTION REFRAMED

For much of my life, rejection felt like a verdict, proof that I was not enough, not chosen, not worthy. Every closed door felt personal. Every no confirmed the fear I already carried inside. Rejection once shaped how I saw myself, how I served, and how I pursued purpose.

But restoration changed my perspective.

Today, I no longer see rejection as abandonment. I see it as divine intervention.

Rejection is God's protection.

I now understand that some doors did not close because I lacked value but because God was protecting me from environments, relationships, and assignments that would have compromised my peace, identity, or destiny. God is omnipresent, and He can see what we cannot. He knows what will drain us, delay us, or derail us. Rejection became one of the ways He guarded my heart and preserved my calling. What once felt like loss, I now know was God shielding me.

Rejection is God's redirection.

Rejection is also one of God's most effective tools for redirection. When I could not hear Him clearly through comfort, He allowed discomfort to move me. When I grew attached to people, places, and roles that were no longer aligned, rejection nudged me forward. I used to interpret rejection as failure. I now know God was repositioning me and ordering my steps with His will. Every closed door pointed me toward a door I would not have chosen for myself, but one that ultimately led to greater wholeness. Scripture tells us,

The steps of a good man
are ordered by the LORD.
(Psalm 37:23 NKJV)

Building Endurance, Not Avoidance

One of the greatest lessons my restoration process taught me is that healing does not mean the absence of rejection; it means the absence of its power over me. I no longer run from rejection, nor do I chase acceptance. Instead, I have learned to endure rejection without allowing it to wound my identity. I built tolerance—not hardness of heart but strength of spirit. I learned to feel rejection without internalizing it.

Why? Because I am already accepted.

I no longer seek validation from people because my identity is anchored in God. When rejection comes, it no longer defines me; it simply informs me. It tells me where I am not assigned, not aligned, or not needed. And that is okay.

If God is for us, who can be against us?
(Romans 8:31 NIV)

Rejection no longer sends me into retreat. It sends me into prayer. It no longer silences me. It sharpens my discernment. It no longer strips me of confidence. It reminds me that I belong to God first.

Living Free from the Fear of Rejection

Rejection once controlled my decisions. Now, it no longer gets a vote. I am free to obey God without needing approval. Free to walk away without explanation. Free to remain whole even when misunderstood. Free to serve from overflow not from insecurity.

Restoration taught me this truth: Rejection cannot remove what God has established. What God accepts, no one can reject. And that is where I now stand—whole, secure, and unshaken. I move forward with courage, consistency, and confidence.

The process of restoration is worth more than silver or gold. I am the wealthiest woman in the world—not because of what I possess but because of who I am in Him.

I am restored.

I am aligned.

I am whole.

And I am forever changed.

REFLECTION

What has God restored in me through this journey?
How will I live differently because of what God has healed?
Where is God sending me next—with this restored identity?

BIBLICAL TRUTH TO CARRY

Be encouraged that "*he who began a good work in you will carry it on to completion* (Philippians 1:6 NIV).

CLOSING PRAYER

Abba Father,
Thank You for revealing truth to my heart and for meeting me where I am. I surrender every area of my life fully to You and thank You for healing what has been wounded. Realign my heart with Your will and help me walk in obedience and trust You in every area of my life. I receive Your grace, restoration, and peace today. In the name of Jesus, amen.

ENDNOTES

[1] "Rejection," Cambridge Dictionary, https://dictionary.cambridge.org/us/dictionary/english/rejection.

[2] "Re," Merriam-Webster.com, https://www.merriam-webster.com/dictionary/re.

[3] "Re," Membean, https://membean.com/roots/re-back.

[4] "Repent," Merriam-Webster, https://www.merriam-webster.com/dictionary/repent.

[5] "Redeem," Merriam-Webster, https://www.merriam-webster.com/dictionary/redeem.

[6] "Cether 5643," Bible Hub, https://biblehub.com/hebrew/5643.htm.

[7] "This Old House," YouTube.com, https://www.youtube.com/@thisoldhouse.

[8] "Revival," Dictionary.com, https://www.dictionary.com/browse/revival.

[9] "What Is a Soul Injury?" MacyCatheter.com, https://www.macycatheter.com/wp-content/uploads/2018/05/Soul-Injury-Fact-Sheet.pdf.

---

[10] "Reinstall," Collins Dictionary, https://www.collinsdictionary.com/us/dictionary/english/reinstalled.

[11] "Reset," Lingvanex, https://lingvanex.com/dictionary/meaning/english/reset/.

[12] "Renew," Cambridge Dictionary, https://dictionary.cambridge.org/us/dictionary/english/renew.

[13] "Reclaim," Cambridge Dictionary, https://dictionary.cambridge.org/us/dictionary/english/reclaim#google_vignette.

[14] "What Happens When You Drive on Bad Alignment?" Tires Plus, April 20, 2023, https://www.tiresplus.com/blog/alignment/can-you-drive-with-bad-alignment/?srsltid=AfmBOoqbov3Eh17XqwUbsWdaHe1n0OYmOteTxdHmSO06Cf_MCww2W3Re.

[15] "Restore," Cambridge Dictionary, https://dictionary.cambridge.org/us/dictionary/english/restore.

www.ingramcontent.com/pod-product-compliance
Lightning Source LLC
La Vergne TN
LVHW090615110826
845146LV00001B/403

* 9 7 9 8 2 3 4 0 1 7 2 9 1 *